Developing Confidence Within: Awakening your True Being

By: Jon Caranganee

isclaimer: For Education purposes only

Copyright 2022 Jon Caranganee Books

Table of Contents:

- Intro
- A Glimpse at my Story
- Confidence is fragile
- Confidence gained not overnight
- Confidence Building Tips
- Happiness fulfills us
- Maintaining Confidence in your Daily Life
- Confident only at certain times
  - Value Yourself
  - Don't Overthink
- Labels are meaningless without the actions
- When she backs away
- She says she's not interested in you or dating anyone
- Never get jealous
- The many layers of a relationship
- Laughter is Mutual
- Public Confidence
- Eating healthy exercising confidence
- Focusing on accomplishments positive and negative results
- Fake it until you make it to gain confidence in Public
- As people we are very stubborn when it comes to learning new things. Sometimes we'll trot and fail and do our things around us besides changing who we are.
- No one values your accomplishments but you
- Relatable people bond. work/daily life
- Forget the hi's and goodbyes to see their reaction
- Humans are lazy. Disabled individuals have more ambitions and do more in their lives than abled body people.
- Don't overthink thought that might not come true
- Revealing apparel brings wrongful attention
- Remove yourself to see if others miss you

- Breathing and Pausing breeds confidence
- Having around bad influential people can affect you
- Mastering something new in life (work)
- You can be affected only by what you let affect you
- Confidence Overlapping personal, work
- Negative role models have negative effects
- We love to see the change but we hate making changes
- Confidence will rain out of you when you're at the top of your game
- Impress yourself
- Positive music helps (gospel, uplifting)
- Don't be controlled by your habits.
- I froze up when I saw a Person of Interest
- What to say to someone I don't know
- Once a week rule
- I wish I would've took that change (talking to someone or doing something)
- Stand up for yourself
- Why don't people talk to me
- Why girls don't talk to me
- It's not you
- Happiness's true meaning
  - Meeting Someone
- Living in True Confidence
  - Saying One-Liners
- Pure Joy
- Making New Friends
- The many forms of beauty
- Drawbacks of high expectations
- Taking pressure off yourself when people are pushing you
- Dealing with negative people it's never right or good enough.
- Be Energized
- Hearing and understanding make people more open to you.
- Valuing your work over your health.
- Why don't they listen to me and want to hear and understand

me?
- The weak never get valued
- No one wants to hear your excuses
- Being unique and different stands out
- Don't be afraid to ask questions
- Never underestimate Anyone
- Live in reality not fantasy
- Someone's always going to try to one up you
- Are you attracting people around you and inviting them through body language
- You can't take back what you say
- Employees value your boss and bosses value your employees.
- Not everyone is going to like you.
- Don't get hung up

- Asking for Forgiveness and walking away
- Don't Judge people based on Looks
- Don't bribe people into liking you
- Getting out of our shell is the hardest thing to do.
- Doing nothing gets you nowhere
- Conclusion:

Intro

 I'm glad you took the time to decide to take the next step in life and develop confidence within you. Confidence is a must if you want good success. It can be very hard to live life without confidence. I know I've been there so many times in my life when I couldn't understand confidence and how it could make my life better. Reading this book will help you gain the confidence you deserve in your life. I encourage you since the human mind retains so little information the first read that you would read this book more than once. The more you read it the more you have this information at the front of your mind. Serious learners generally read books at least 10 times.

A Glimpse at my Story:

 I was a shy guy growing up. Thinking hey opportunities will go my way and I'm nice and attractive enough that things will work out fine. But boy was I wrong! I lived my life having moments of being confident and moments where I wasn't confident. Bursting out of my bubble for a while in school got me popular with a lot of people but it felt like a roller coaster. My confidence was high then it dropped and I was an ordinary guy yet again. Tagging along with the popular kids having some moments of shine for me but then just felt like being another follower of everyone else. Senior year I felt on top of the world. Yet it was the best year of my school life (Like most people). I felt confident and things felt amazing. I got the classes I wanted and felt like I could take on the world. After graduating things started to take a different turn in my life. I worked with my father on the family farm thinking I could take over one day. Thinking it'd be great to be my own boss and live life my way without answering to a boss and progressive in life for the things I wanted. Then when the market crashed my only option was to get a job. I started working at different jobs and my shy, young, submissive behavior is what caused me to think that I didn't deserve to negotiate for wages. I started working at a material handling company but being in the upper midwest and getting hired on an outdoor job when there was -60 degree below windchill and operating a cabless forklift with no heat it wasn't ideal. I lasted a week and a half before I quit. I didn't even have the guts to tell them directly to put my notice in. I left a note with the receptionist. I came to find out that no one got the note because the receptionist quit before I did and I told them I was quitting the same day. So, then I said to myself I deserve a better job than that (Especially with heat!). I went around applying and my second job I applied for called me and wanted me to work for them. I negotiated the wage the same as the last job when I could have got more (I was desperate for a job). I then got the job and started working. It felt good at first I got a cool job making custom parts for skid steers but I was incompetent at certain things and wasn't the most confident. I worked there for a month and the first job I applied at called back and wanted to give me an interview. I passed the interview with flying colors but wasn't sure I wanted the job. I then got an offer in the mail and then I jumped onto the opportunity and started making almost double my wage. Life went on and I went through more jobs and then I found that I had high notes and bumps in the road of my life.

Confidence is fragile

Is confidence really fragile? The answer is Yes! It is very fragile, especially at first. The thing is that we can feel on top of the world and then feel like at the bottom of the pit in our confidence level. We often think that confidence is like a rock and it cannot be taken away and things will always be good for the confident individual. After all these life coaches and people tell you just to be yourself and be confident but they never tell you how to really be confident! It's sad because confidence is such an important aspect in our life but we never learn the right way to be confident and how to sustain confidence. If we continue to lack confidence we will never become confident. The more you become less confident. It's like a hole that gets deeper.

Confidence gained not overnight

Confidence is not something that will happen in a shear second. It takes a while and it takes time. How your body language and mindset are will reflect on the duration in which confidence will be gained. For example if you're nervous and wanting to get that job you always wanted. You may experience butterflies in the stomach and feel intimidated thinking you might not measure up or get the job. This is why gaining confidence is not an overnight strategy. It takes time and the only way to get through is to do what is uncomfortable. Though it may seem hard at first, doing more of what makes you uncomfortable is what will make you successful. It's hard to believe I've been there. In fact, the companies I wanted to work for I felt that exact feeling. I even drove beyond the company because I was intimidated and had stomach knots. But I calmed myself down and went there and talked. I didn't get the job right away and left my information but a few weeks went by and then I got the job! I made family members and friends jealous of my occupation at that time! It felt great and I was glad I made that decision to get the courage to drive in and walk in that door. I was scared to face rejection but I knew if I didn't go for it I would regret it by not getting the job I truly desired and was passionate about. This is what happens if you take that risk of getting rejected. If you don't you will never know what you want in life or what you could have experienced because you will be too scared.

Confidence Building Tips

Think of ways you can build your confidence. One good way is to build goals in your daily life. Small or big it doesn't matter just as long as you feel productive in your daily life. Sitting on the couch and playing video games and ranking up in the game may feel accomplished but here's the thing. You accomplished in the video game but you didn't accomplish anything in your life. Or you may have watched all the seasons of a popular T.V. show and know it by heart but guess what it may help to have conversations with other people who watch the same show but you still didn't accomplish things to make your own life better. Remember big goals take time to reach sometimes. So if you fail then try again or try a different method or approach. The problem is many people give up before they actually become good at something or accomplish something. Becoming amazing in life takes time and many people aren't amazing overnight, sometimes it takes a decade! Another good way is to be a person of your word. If you don't follow through in trying to keep your word it becomes meaningless. When others can rely upon you it makes you feel good inside because it brings value to yourself. It shows that others value you as well and can build your confidence. Becoming solid in life is what can make you more confident as well. If you care about what others think of you it can hurt and affect yourself. If your co-worker tells you you're worthless and you believe it then you will become it. But if you don't let their words impact you then it can make you stronger because it doesn't bother you and you will maintain your confidence level. It's easier said than done because at that point in your life it can be hard to actually be deflecting negative actions and words that are thrown at you personally. As humans we take things personally and when you do it will hurt your core essence and confidence. If you continue to take these negative beatings it will lower your confidence in a hurry. So what do I do when someone says something negative towards me. I'll either laugh it up or think of something else. "Remember you can only let others affect you if you allow it." But if you wrecked something more serious at work this is tougher to actually practice. Then if this happens I will simply say everything is going to be okay. Be reasonable in your statement and be honest. You may lose your job but your integrity is so much more important. There will be another job waiting for you but if you lie about it. It may prolong your work life but what happens if you get caught in that lie. Then you'll lose your job as well and then if your future job calls about you then they might say you were a dishonest person rather than a person who just made a simple mistake that may have been a career limiting move but then if you had a good work relationship with others and did your job correctly over the course of time then they'll be more likely to hire you even if you were fired. It's harder to get a job if you have a history of theft or dishonesty and you'll be watched more and trusted less.

Happiness fulfills us

Do what makes you happy in life. If you're passionate about something or a a hobby you love to do then it can make it easier to build your confidence as well. It can help regain your confidence and happiness in your life by doing things That make you happy. It works great in this way because your happy zone is your break zone. It can clear your mind and help you think clearly. Tension can hurt your thinking and ways and cripple confidence.

Maintaining Confidence in your Daily Life

If you let your confidence dwindle it will fall. The thing I found out about confidence is that it's perishable. If you don't remain confident and do things that breed confidence then it will fall. I found that out the hard way. I would bounce between being very confident and then being not confident. You need to get to a place in your life where you can be confident no matter what.

Confident only at certain times

So, you're thinking what the title of this paragraph actually means or maybe you can relate with this topic. Confidence can be noted at times when you feel like you're confident when you're on top of your game at work and helping others but when you're out and about on your own you lose confidence or when you're starting a new job. If you feel this way it's perfectly normal. Because when your incompetent you're not confident. Competence breeds confidence.

Value Yourself

Truth is that if you don't value yourself no one else will value you. What you see yourself is how others will see you. It comes to show that even if you come off as weak, willing, or submissive to people they still won't respect you. People only tend to value themselves and will take you for granted in general. Most people who will value you tend to be friends and family. The only way to get people to actually value you is to in turn value yourself. This reminds me of my life personally. I would go along with the flow of things at work just to have a peaceful work environment. I was shy and didn't speak up for myself as much as

I should have. This resulted in others not respecting me to my desires. People may feel you're too easy and **will** take advantage of you. But you need to take a stand but don't be trying to get into a fight but rather set boundaries that are within reason that most people don't do. Otherwise people will run over you like an animal crossing the road.

Don't Overthink

As people we tend to overthink certain details in our life. Like especially how others view us. We tend to put more onto others and how they view us instead of thinking of how we view them. We often think when there is a group of people and we're left out wondering if they are talking about you behind your back. Although it could be true and sometimes it isn't it tends to pull away confidence. When we're thinking this way it can be toxic to the mind because we need to think if they're talking about me. You can't be bothered by it. If you're bothered by it you're giving them power and letting it bother you which in turn makes you weaker. I've been here before as well as other people so if this is you then you're not alone! Unless you're doing something immoral I would not worry about them and try to focus on you and what you are currently doing.

Labels are meaningless without the actions

Many people think that just because you have a label on something has meaning but without the actions the words are meaningless. Think of people who say they're your friend but do they really act as your friend? Never put a label on things when it comes to women at all! Labeling is up to the girl not the guy. Because once you put a label on it some women will get offended if a guy puts a label on them and may cause her to back away. Your job as a man is to have both of you to have a great time and fun. Nothing more nothing less.

When she backs away

When a girl backs away it means you're either pursuing her too much or she's testing to see if you'll over pursue her too much. Remember don't over do it. Conversation is a game of tennis. If you're hitting the ball too much and it's not coming back, you don't keep on running after the ball. So many times guys will over do this and ruin their chances with the girl. Never do this! Never bring emotions into texting or the phone call **Ever!** If you do it will end very badly. Girls are emotional beings and men are logic and reason beings. Girls will throw emotions into the conversation and make matters worse for you. So if she backs away then you will back away. Repeat what she's doing. If she doesn't reach out for a while, give it some time. So, if she doesn't respond after a day, give her some time to reach out. Maybe wait half a week to a week. Then ask how she's doing. If you're in a dating relationship with her then when you contact her setup a time to meet up with her and see her again. If she declines then ask her to get in touch with you when she's free to get together. The thing is get your life together and have things going on in your life. It keeps you occupied so you're not obsessing over them. If you obsess over them it will make them back away from you and possibly make them avoid you. Never overdo it! Be patient and take it slow. Never rush things otherwise it can make her back away from you.

She says she's not interested in you or dating anyone

You may have run across a girl who says i'm not interested in dating you or into the dating scene. Truth is she might be actually saying what she means but then again she might not. Women will say these things to nudge a guy off her. It helps her by not dealing with an over emotional guy who is on her like a cheap suit. I ran across this before when a girl told me this and I thought to myself what gives? She said she's not interested in dating anyone and wants to remain single. I couldn't get over the fact that she said this same thing. I thought I'm an attractive guy with good qualities. What gives? Some years later she was onto the dating scene and I was thinking to myself why did she say she didn't wasn't interested in dating even though now she is? Well, I came to the conclusion that women say things they particularly don't mean and minds do change overtime. She enjoyed weddings, kids, and talked about getting married one day and then she says she's not into dating and wanting to get involved. It seemed really contradictory. This is why when women say things never take it to heart 100%. Instead be optimistic and you never know, maybe it might work out in the future!

Never get jealous

People tend to get jealous in their daily lives. Whether it's at work, friends, family, or a significant other. Jealousy can get us in trouble in a lot of ways and it leads to revenge or getting back at them. Now using that and trying to outdo someone can lead to great inventions with competition. It can help make us strive harder to do more to better ourselves and show that we can do more. But I'm talking about if you are seeing a girl and she's not paying attention to you or if a guy isn't paying attention to you then you go out with someone else.Then you text them or send them a picture of yourself with someone else to make them jealous. Or if you are with another person trying to make them jealous. Guys and girls do this oftentimes. This is not healthy because then it goes back and forth. She might find another guy to do the same thing with and it just keeps going and the problem is that in all honesty it's pretty childish. The truth is you're either in or you're out. You shouldn't try to get someone jealous as a tactic to get someone back because it doesn't end in a good way. It comes down to if the person takes your time for granted and they disrespect you and your time then it's time to move on. If they want you back then let them make it up to you, if you want them back. Because if they are the ones to break it off with you then it's their turn to make it up with you. While in the meantime you should be working on yourself to become a better version of who you are instead of trying to play games.

The many layers of a relationship

When people think of a relationship they tend to think that it's all just about getting along and loving each other but it's more than just that. Yes, it's essential but if you peel a relationship to see what's really in it you'll see that there's more to it than that.

Here are some examples:
1. Knowing how that person feels or acts in certain situations whenever something comes up good or bad.

2. Seeing how that person actually feels and does for you by actions not words.
3. Not letting others influence the decision about your relationship and neither one is affected by this.

4. Always loving each other no matter what in sickness and health.

5. Always trustworthy, faithful and loyal.

6. Loves to be in your presence.

7. Seeing if that person is a giver or a taker in their daily actions.

8. Values your opinion

9. Laughs at your stupid jokes and never gets tired of them.

10. Open her up, talk to her, and get her happy again when she is angry and non-talkative.

11. Being a good parent with discipline by both parents not

giving in.

12. Ability to be in love for many years through hardships and good times.

Laughter is Mutual

Think of it in this way. Laughter is something that can be universal or it can be closed in which others will not join in laughter even though it is a funny statement or action. Why you may ask, well it's because it's the relationship you have with that individual. People like comedians have people who don't laugh at their jokes neither. Why because people may not find them funny or it could be that the person might not be interested in them or have any mutual liking towards them. Take an instance where someone in a friends group can say something that's not really funny but others are laughing anyhow and the reason for this is the mutual interest or liking towards that person. The rapport you have with someone can sometimes dictate humor with them. Like when a girl who likes you will laugh at your stupid corny jokes because she likes you. Another reason why confidence is needed is because you could tell a joke that is funny but then crickets start to creak in the dead silence of those around you. So learn some funny lines like "I thought that was going to get a better response." or "You guys are making this awkward with your silence" But do it in a funny and joking tone of voice. It's all about how you present it to others. If you would have a tone and body language of uncomfort it makes it more awkward yet because of the way it's being presented.

Public Confidence

Public confidence is something that we must get good at if we wish to see great results when we go out into public events. I know people who fear large crowds that are afraid or self conscious around people. The more time you spend in isolation or separation from people starts to take away our nature of being social. With the pandemic a lot of people faced this but society tends to be anti-social even though we have social media it tends to make us less social in the outside world. If we wish to get confident we have to overcome the fear. What I recommend is simple. Go to a public event and use a tip that some people overlook. Are you ready for it? Accessories such as Sunglasses or a hat. When you're at an outdoor event this helps quite a bit. Because people can't see who you are and it doesn't matter how you appear because your face is hidden. But also know that most people don't even know who you are. So then it doesn't matter what others think of you because no one knows or cares who you are. Therefore you are free to gain confidence in this particular setting and overcome fear.

Eating healthy exercising confidence

It's interesting how people eat. Some people are overweight and the things they grab in the store are cheese balls and cotton candy and that's it! This is where confidence can lay down in a negative way because if you're eating unhealthy it's going to make you feel unhealthy. If you eat healthy it makes you feel healthy. Cotton candy and cheese balls may taste really good if you indulge in it too much but it'll have a negative effect on your body. Let's face it, we tend to be self conscious about our weight and it can make us feel a lack of confidence. When I workout I tend to feel better and more confident in myself.

Focusing on accomplishments positive and negative results

Focusing on your accomplishments can have a negative effect on your mind. Now keep in mind it can definitely have a positive effect on confidence but what tends to happen is that we tend to embellish in our accomplishments. Which in turn makes you lazy and thinking to yourself that you're high above. This has a negative effect because of the complacent habits it forms. Which is why your mindset should be the most productive way you can spend your time and live your life. Otherwise you'll go nowhere when you live in the moment of basking in your accomplishments. Note your accomplishments and how they helped you and made you feel great in that moment but keep moving forward otherwise you'll go nowhere.

Fake it until you make it to gain confidence in Public

When you're out in public by yourself and you feel alone and insecure the best thing to do is to fake in your mind that you're popular or pretend that you're taken or in a relationship. This can be hard because it's not always easy to actually do this. But if you master this it can make it easy to gain confidence.

As people we are very stubborn when it comes to learning new things. Sometimes we'll trot and fail and do our things around us besides changing who we are.

As people we can be very stubborn. We don't want to take time to learn new things in life but rather watch T.V., play video games, or do something non productive. It is easier to sit back and not do anything in life but the rewards are not by any means great. You generally won't advance in your career or life. Now doing more does take more and has failures but if you don't press on you won't ever see the finish line in life and ever overcome the hardships to actually see the reward that is bestowed unto you.

No one values your accomplishments but you

We often think that winning that trophy or winning it big is going to impress everyone. But in reality what I learned is that the people who value your accomplishments are mainly you. Now, friends or family might be supportive of your winning and be encouraging to you but the meaning is more to you than to them unless it's a team effort.

Relatable people bond. work/daily life

You ever notice that you might be the odd person out when it comes to conversation with others. But the truth is that if you don't build rapport with anyone or listen to them they may be more distant to you. Remember if you're distant to them they will be distant to you. What I recommend is to be what you need to be. If you're genuinely interested in that person as they are with you then it will create a bond or a real connection but you shouldn't try to fake your interest in someone to take advantage of them. What you should do is be kind and nice to them but don't let them take advantage of you. Because people will generally take advantage of you and take you for granted. That is why nice guys finish last as they say because they tend to be pushovers that can be taken advantage of by other people and used, which is not what you want to be. Now, helping people is a different concern and being nice is not a bad thing but letting people take advantage of you is unhealthy and bad for your self esteem.

Forget the hi's and goodbyes to see their reaction

If you want to see if people pay attention to your presence the best method I use is to forget saying hi and goodbye to them. When you do this you end up removing your attention and seeing if people have any rapport built up with you. Let them be the first to make the gesture of a hi or goodbye. Sometimes people are busy so there are exceptions but if they never make the effort then you'll know. Most generally I found at work they sometimes had a 50/50 motive where I would have to say it first and then they would and other times they would bring it up. But pay attention to those who say it more often towards you. Then you'll find out who is liking you more. Now this is a very subtle way of doing things but it can help you determine people's liking towards you.

Humans are lazy. Disabled individuals have more ambitions and do more in their lives than abled body people.

It's sad to see this but it's true. I see Disabled individuals being more successful than able bodied people. They know of their disability but they choose to press on knowing that they want to be just as important as everyone else and not left out. It's truly amazing when I saw and knew people who had a disadvantage but became so successful and full of life. It made me realize that we take our abilities for granted and get lazy which is so unfortunate because I see people saying that success isn't for me but it is you just have to work for it and it will come. Sometimes it takes a decade but the winners circle is so small because people I don't want to put the extra effort in life.

Don't overthink thought that might not come true

We often think that we picture ourselves with that job we dream of or that particular person we wish to spend the rest of our life with and think of our future. But truth be told it is a bad way to think because it puts expectation on it and when it doesn't happen it brings us down. We can't put the carriage before the horse in life. If we do then failures are sure to happen. We need to think in the mindset of having potential goals of having a great job or a future with someone but not to pin it on one particular place or person. Rather take it one day at a time without regret. That no matter what I'll make a good decision and someday that will come true for me.

Revealing apparel brings wrongful attention

Many people sometimes like to wear revealing apparel that shows too much skin and may attract wrongful attention. I know people who are way too young wearing

this kind of apparel and can get themselves in a load of issues and trouble. If you want to bring rightful attention in your life you need to dress appropriately! After all you want people with meaning coming up to you and not those who are focused primarily on your body. Generally they don't have you in mind rather their own desires that can cause a lot of turmoil and usery. Then, they'll toss you off to the side and look for someone else. Attract people in your life who are attracted to you from a normal standpoint and not a revealing standpoint.

Remove yourself to see if others miss you

If you feel like others aren't giving you attention and don't care then remove your attention. If it gets results then they have interest and care but if they don't then it shows their lack of interest which isn't good! Now sometimes people are busy in their lives and don't show the proper attention to you but people who are close to

you don't show the attention or give you the time of day for you then remove yourself from them. It shows quickly if they value you. If you have so-called friends who call themselves your good friends and don't care if they see you or not then it shows that their words are meaningless because their actions are saying the opposite. In an ideal state you want people who are excited and happy to see you! Not feeling obligated to having to spend time with you.

Breathing and Pausing breeds confidence

Ever feel rushed to talk to someone you're interested in or at a job you really want but are nervous? The best thing is to calm yourself by breathing slowly and relaxing. Pausing to not run your words together or at a fast rate. Going fast then you will have likely chances of ruining that opportunity. We give others more time to speak than we do ourselves. You need to be happy whether you get that phone number or that job opportunity that you will be strong enough that you can be strong before and after that interview because if you aren't then things won't be the same for you and you'll crumble.

Having around bad influential people can affect you

Negative people are always a buzz kill. They will often take you for granted and may use you in a negative way that will hurt you or get you in trouble with authorities. You need to remove those people from your life otherwise they will drag you down. If they are family you need to set healthy boundaries with them saying I can't be around you if you keep acting like this. They need to feel the pain if they don't change their negative habits so that the consequences are real.

Mastering something new in life (work)

We tend to want to be masters in our jobs. Even when we first start, the truth is that it takes time. Being great at something takes time but sometimes we wish to be great on the first day. I remember starting a new job. I wanted to be the best at what I did. It can be frustrating because you truly want to be good at what you do and make very few mistakes but oftentimes it doesn't work like this unfortunately. You tend to learn after your mistakes and it can be a big mistake depending on which can really take your confidence on a downward spiral. But unfortunately our big mistakes can help us change who we are with big consequences that can cause someone to get fired.

You can be affected only by what you let affect you

Remember people can only affect you whenever you let it affect you! People will always try to be negative and put you down. It does hurt but if you let it get to you then they win. You have officially given them power over you. Don't do it because it will drag you down and affect you in a negative aspect. Don't dwell or think about their hateful comment but think of something else. Distract your mind with something else and think happy thoughts.

Confidence Overlapping personal, work

If you have confidence in your personal life it can overlap with your work life and vice versa. But remembering a bad day at work can also drop your confidence. So don't let it get to you even though it can be pretty bad at some work places. Trust me I've been there!

Negative role models have negative effects

Look at some of these celebrities and their negative influences on millions if not more. It's Sad to see so many people taken by these people and they have nothing but unhealthy lifestyles that make society so evil and provocative. By saying it's okay but really it's not and because their famous people follow them not for what they represent the lavish living they have. It disgusts me to see these people leading people astray from their true calling in life.

We love to see the change but we hate making changes

We often want to see change but we don't want to make the effort to make change in life. We sit around thinking things will change someday if we just sit back. That change will be a negative one and you'll regret not having done things sooner in life to be farther in life than you are currently!

Confidence will rain out of you when you're at the top of your game

Confidence rains out of you when you are the best at your job and on top of your life. When you get so good at a job and if you love and feel good about your job you tend to have so much confidence. People see and feel that vibe you give out and will generally ask you for guidance. I always loved being in this position. It felt so natural. But when you switch to a different job it can change because it'll be something new and it'll take time to get there and sometimes you'll have to leave that job to find what you desire and what actually is best for you.

Impress yourself

Impress yourself rather than others. We often take time to impress others without valuing ourselves. It's a sad reality that we do tend to value others more than ourselves. We often care more about our job or other's perception about us. In reality we should focus on our happiness and what makes us who we are. We tend to forget because we spend more time on other things. The problem is that people who don't value themselves aren't valued by others and it can drag you down.

Positive music helps (gospel, uplifting)

Music affects our mood swings. I tend to have found that gospel and uplifting music helped me feel encouraged and lifted me up. Now coming from a religious and spiritual background I tend to listen to gospel and it does work if you allow it. But the key essence is to surround yourself with this uplifting music to help drain the negative day away and it helps put you back on track in life when you need it the most.

Don't be controlled by your habits.

We as humans become controlled by our very habits and it can be very negative because you fall into a trance of doing the same thing day and night. It sucks because our day is controlled by this and we don't get anything else done. It can affect you greatly and sometimes cause a negative spiral in life. You need to change it up by doing something different even if you're uncomfortable. You need to make good, healthy decisions that will help you grow as a person.

I froze up when I saw a Person of Interest

When you see an attractive person and you freeze it can have repercussions. It can cause you not to have the opportunity of meeting that particular person or messing it up. You need to feel as though I could live without them. You need to feel as if you're the prize in life. This is where a bit of cockiness is important, not overdoing it but enough to keep those fearful feelings away.

What to say to someone I don't know

When you're at a store or out and you see someone and you wish to talk to them. Remember they might not be in the mood to talk. Be friendly with an opener like how are you doing?; how's your day going tell me about it?; or make an appropriate funny comment and ask for their name. Don't be scared even if the conversation goes south, learn from it and improve on it. That's why you practice this to perfect your skills.

Once a week rule

Here's something I did to help my confidence. I went out at least once a week if not more. Go shopping or out to eat and converse with people. Get used to being around others and it will help you gain confidence and get used to talking to people so it becomes natural. Challenge yourself and those you feel uncomfortable talking to because of their beauty or if they look grouchy. Sometimes they still might be grouchy or sometimes you'll brighten their day. But don't let the grouchy people ruin or rain on your day otherwise it can affect confidence. Have the attitude that I could take it or leave it if they choose to talk to me.

I wish I would've took that change (talking to someone or doing something)

Taking charge and changing in life is difficult. Moments when you didn't take that opportunity and now you're in regret. Trust me I've been there multiple times and it is not a pleasant feeling not to have taken that chance and opportunity could have awaited me. There are times when I did step out of my comfort zone and did take that approach but other times I have let those moments pass and I regret them. I ask you not to do the same. You might've already and it eats at you and sometimes it's good to have patience in other decisions but when fear strikes and you freeze up and wait on that opportunity it becomes a hard moment for all of us to actually face. Maybe it was a business opportunity or a romantic interest in someone and it got hesitated and maybe that business opportunity or potential a person of interest found someone else. Now in certain cases it may be for the best but the point is knowing that it was right for you without a doubt and you passed on it made it regretful. Don't be that way! Sometimes it's good to wait on decisions, especially big ones but if you ever have nerves in your body and you know for a fact that it's a good decision, don't hold back but go for it. Otherwise regret will enter your mind. Now, tomorrow is a new day and the biggest thing to do is learn from it and not to take things too hard but to examine what you could have done and when an opportunity strikes in the future you will be ready!

Stand up for yourself

People will take advantage of you until you stand up for yourself. Oftentimes we think that going with the flow will make people like you but people will often take you for granted. It's sad but it's the way things are with this. You'd think that going with what people say at work and minding your own business would make the workplace better. It may make it smoother and more pleasant to work in a sense, well possibly but you're not being true to yourself and it makes you feel unhappy or lacking because you didn't stand up for what is actually right to you or showing how you really feel. Now, creating a hostile workplace because you but heads with everyone is not ideal either. It creates tension in the workplace and people will dislike you and possibly you might get fired for it as well. You want to make a smooth work environment but speak your mind in a good way and don't get down when others try to make you feel this way. It may require some time to rewrite your mind to not let others bother you but once you do it makes everything better.

Why don't people talk to me

You might be one of those who think why aren't people talking to me when I'm out at a public place. Well, let me tell you about my experience. Sometimes when I was out I was sitting by the bar just watching a football game but wanted to enjoy the company of others. I was outgoing but others were not wanting to talk to me much. So now you're asking what gives and what did I do wrong? Here is my explanation on the subject. Others may want to talk to you while others do not want to talk to you. But the best thing to do is maintain the attitude of not caring what others think of you. But here's more to the story: I started talking to a gentleman who was eating and asked him about what he was eating. Later, I noticed his motorcycle apparel and asked him about owning a motorcycle and what kind he owned and which one he enjoyed the most. Then, as time went by he then asked about where I lived. So, now you see in this example I had to ask multiple times about him before he even inquired anything about me. If you don't succeed, keep trying. Remember some people have to be opened up. Others may open up sooner than others but if you keep on with a positive and nothing to lose attitude that is where you want to be.

Why girls don't talk to me

Now, you're wondering what happens if a girl I like doesn't talk to me then what? Here's the essence: some women will be more wanting to talk to you than others. Some may have interest right off the bat and some you'll have to talk to open her up or some simply wish not to have anything to do with you. Here's an example: I was out one night and I met some ladies who worked there. It was noisy and loud and it can be very hard to have a conversation which doesn't work to your advantage one bit. Later that night it started getting calmer and more quiet, which is an ideal way to have conversations. One girl was easy to open up and I started talking to her and we started hitting it off and made a connection and the other was a lot harder to open up but then again she was busy. But remember girls or guys who like you will make more time to want to take their time and spend it with you. Now the girl who was harder to open up didn't care much for my small talk while the other girl enjoyed my company and small talk. The girl who was harder to talk to after I started opening her up and getting her talking about herself and her likes and interests she then started being friendly towards me and interested. Remember to ask a girl what her name is first without volunteering your own then if she asks your name then you know that she has some interest towards you. Both girls by the way asked for my name. Although the conversation was so much smoother for the girl who was easier to talk to and it made it more enjoyable for the conversation. Easy and effortless conversations and interactions with women are ideal. It makes the experience so much better. You have to spend a lot of time and effort to get them to have interest in you. Now, my intention wasn't to get their numbers or information but simply to go out and have a good time. You shouldn't have the intention of getting a girl's number but you should always have the intention of just having a good time. Otherwise it can ruin your confidence if all you're focused on is getting someone's number and then it can really make it harder when they decline to give you their information.

It's not you

Remember when people don't communicate with you or smile at you when you're out somewhere and they smile and talk to someone else. They look at you with a weird look of unhappiness like what are you looking at don't take it personally some people are going to be into you some aren't.

Happiness's true meaning

Happiness is a feeling granted when you have happiness in your life everything else in life goes better. You can have an amazing job but if you're not happy in your job it's going to make your job worse. You can't really fake the feelings of happiness if you're not happy you will never be happy. You want to have to seek happiness in order to find happiness in your life whatever you do whatever you accomplish and whatever you're going for in life

Meeting Someone

You'll never meet the man or woman of your dreams if you stay at home. Think of it this way: you're a walking billboard. You're advertising yourself whenever you go out. You're going to advertise yourself to other potential people that you might have an interaction with or possible future relationship or anything of that notion. If you don't take that chance granted there are dating websites which do work there's other things as well but you need to be on the move if you want to groove.

Living in True Confidence

When you live in confidence you live in true happiness. When you feel like you're in your own Aura your own world and nothing can penetrate your bubble of happiness. It can be one of the best things in life and that's what you want to experience. You don't want things that can easily take you down, you want to be strong and you need to get to a point in your life in your confidence in walking within yourself that you're comfortable being you and you can be outgoing and have happiness pour out of you. Remember the person who's having a good time is the one people are going to go up to because the one who's having a good time is a happy fun person. If you're being shy and unsupportive and just in your safe zone no one is going to want to be around that kind of person.

Saying One-Liners

One liner may be fun but some people do not like one liners. So you have to take it with a grain of salt. If someone's body language or personally tells you that they don't like your one liner just say, well that went over like a lead balloon or I guess I was expecting a bigger reaction. The thing is don't get carried away on a one liner. It's better to build rapport before you use a one liner but some people may be fine saying one liner opener and people responding to it in a positive fashion. It all depends on your skill level as well.

Pure Joy

Pure joy is what can determine happiness and drive in your daily life. Besides eating healthy this can help boost energy in a great way. Which is what the creator said in Nehemiah 8:10 saying the joy of the lord is my strength. I know for me spiritual speaking God's joy is something that lives within and drives me. But if you're not into the God scene which I encourage others to partake in then I recommend you to find something that gives you Joy in life that can help bring you up. If you don't have Joy in your life then life is going to be hard for you because things we are passionate about helps us get through bad days. For example , I love helping people and being a positive influence to others. Which is one of the main reasons I'm writing the short book. I want you to grow and prosper to become something great and a light to others who don't possess Joy and Love in their life.

Making New Friends

This book discussed earlier that taking interest in people makes it easier to make friends and you can actually decide whether or not you're interested in them. The best way to make new friends is obviously by putting yourself out there. Asking them questions about them, think of what makes you want to be friends with them. Are they fun, easy going, and have integrity?

The many forms of beauty

Being attractive is not only looks but personality and desire. I can tell you many Sometimes women or men will actually overlook someone's qualities for a short time because of attraction. But what I found as many people would agree is that beauty is not only on the outside but on the inside as well. I can give an example of a woman I was interested in. She was a beautiful woman but the the way her body language was and how she treated other people made me un-attracted to her. So, in life there's a lot more to a person than just looks! The way they act, treat, and care for you as well as others is vital.

Drawbacks of high expectations

Ever feel like people are always holding you to a high expectation? When you make your mark and now the bar of expectation is raised. Sometimes being an overachiever is a great thing and showing others that you can do a job better or faster can be rewarding but remember drawbacks keep people expecting it all the time. Now, keep in mind you always want to be improving yourself and making a name for yourself but don't let people push you so hard that it hurts your health and exhausts mental capacity in your brain.

Taking pressure off yourself when people are pushing you

When people are expecting high expectations or if you are performing tasks a bit too slow. It happens and it sucks because you want to be at a pace you're comfortable at rather than at a high speed pace that you aren't comfortable working. Some people get fired for not being fast enough and others who make a lot of mistakes by going fast tend to get fired too. The best thing to do is to make yourself feel better by retaining confidence in where you are currently. It's hard to but if others can puncture your confidence bubble then they will be successful. You should try to learn and improve your skills so you will get better at your job but you shouldn't let people push you around and scold you all the time. I found that sometimes we lack paying attention to things around us. We tend to overlook what we're doing because we're bored with our jobs and we forget the details of what we're doing. If we forget the details then if someone asks you if something is missing or where are the parts for so and so or if you gave a task for someone to do. Then the boss comes back with a different problem because something got lost in translation and you don't have an answer to back it up because you weren't paying attention. I've been here before and it isn't pretty. But if you have the details and thoughts collected then it puts you in a higher power. Think of it this way: if a lawyer is lacking details in your case and doesn't pay attention to anything of what he's defending you in then the lawyer is worseless and it makes it bad for you as well. So details in what you do are very important. You can revert back and know for a fact that you did your due diligence. Don't cave and be submissive but stay firm in your answer that you know is 100% correct.

Dealing with negative people it's never right or good enough.

I dealt with people before who no matter what you did it wasn't enough. It's hard to be around them because they take your energy down. They talk negatively about everything and aren't really impressed by the things you do even if it is great work. If you messed up on the job and they bring up the times you messed up the best thing to do is laugh it off. If you let it get to you it will bring you down. You can only be bothered by what you allow to bother you.

Be Energized

Being energized is an important aspect that is often overlooked. Whenever you are out and looking around at other people, what do you see? Are people looking happy, sad, straight faced, non-friendly. When you say hi and smile do they smile back? Did they say hi back or start in a conversation? Sometimes you'll find people who are friendly and some who aren't so friendly and it's common at most places. What you need to be is energized by smiling and saying how are you or how's your day going? See how they act because some people will respond instantly when you do this and others will say nothing and keep on walking or give you a weird look and you know what it's okay! You need to feel comfortable enough to be able to do this. It'll help you gain confidence and not worry about how other people look or if they even respond. Think of it as a burp. It lasts for a short moment and you might get a reaction but then people go on with their lives. Just don't make a big scene then this whole scenario changes. Do what feels naturally healthy and no matter what, stay positive and upbeat.

Hearing and understanding make people more open to you.

When it comes to people we often think of our own agenda and not care so much about others' agenda and lives but the truth is that if you wish for others to take interest in you. Then you must take interest in them. People aren't usually interested in you but they are interested in their own life circle. If you tend to only care about yourself and talk about yourself to other people about how great you are or how great your kids are. Then people are often not interested and they tend not to pay attention to what you're saying. People whom you build rapport with tend to have a high interest in what you do but that's to a certain point. If you're a narcissist then people will usually try to avoid you or make the least amount of conversation possible with you.

Valuing your work over your health.

The long term and short-term effects of doing this

When you value your job more than your health it's going to have a negative effect. There's nothing wrong with being involved with your job and wanting to support yourself or your family. But the truth is that we don't value our health and body enough. We tend to only focus on the job but in reality a job is a job and though it's very important it's best to keep a good job you shouldn't let eating healthier, working out, and releasing stress and tension shouldn't be overlooked. Sometimes we may need to change jobs to actually get to that place in life where It's less stressful and drama free.

Why don't they listen to me and want to hear and understand me?

You can go up to some people and all they talk about is themselves and when you mention things about yourself they could care less or act as if they never heard you. This may come from not having enough rapport or it could be that they are into themselves or narcissists who only care about themselves and no one else. Don't take your time with these people because people who truly want to be with you should actually value you.

The weak never get valued

We often think that if we go along with what everyone else says and does everything will work to our advantage but truth be told is that the weak don't get valued only by people who are strong-willed and non-pushovers. Why?, because they are too easy and are known to be able to be taken advantage of.

No one wants to hear your excuses

You ever run into a situation where you try to make an excuse when you did something and no matter what the excuse was or how justifiable it is people just don't seem to care. It's because people see what you've done and not what you experienced while doing what you were doing. Like for example if you broke something while trying to fix it and it might have been a weak part or something snapped or broken unintentionally but all people see is that you broke it. Doesn't matter if it wasn't your fault they still blame you and it's not a great feeling whatsoever but others will not see this perspective. I always thought if it happened to them it'd change their mind about what i've done but when it happens to them they seem to feel down in the moment when it happens but their ego picks back up a while later. So, what I found is that you'll live in that moment for a while but the feeling will pass and you need to move on. Even if it feels like the end of the world, tomorrow will be a brighter day.

Being unique and different stands out

Unique and different can be a good thing if it's a positive thing. If you use it in a negative reflection it's not ideal because it's how you're making others feel and how they view you. Doing something funny, goofy, and appealing to others is a a great way to meet people or just to make them laugh when they're having a bad day. Now other people might ignore you but you can't let their uptight personality affect you.

Don't be afraid to ask questions
Some are not willing to want to be asked

Being afraid to ask questions in life can have its consequences. I remember not asking questions and ended up struggling so hard when the answer is right around you when the person who knows it may be right next to you. You might have situations in life where you have to figure out the answer but you can save time by asking someone who actually knows the answer. Some people aren't willing to answer questions as much either and it can make a job pretty difficult. I've been there having to figure out issues and problems on my own while having someone who knows the answer is self conceited and doesn't want to share their knowledge to help you or they use their knowledge to make themselves feel power above you.

Never underestimate Anyone

Too many times in life we tend to underestimate people and what they do.

Sometimes giving a person a hard time and making fun of someone can have drastic effects in your personal and work life. Even if they don't seem to be as smart as it may seem they still may know something that you don't know. **Live in reality not fantasy**

Some people live in a world of fantasy. You may be wondering in confusion what this means so simply it means that people sometimes live in a mindset that is thinking that everything is better than what it is and others may see things in a different light that things are worse than they actually are. It's important to live and see everything in the same realm. We tend to make things worse like work when we're there. We tend to think it's terrible that some jobs can be pretty bad, speaking from experience but our mind can make it worse for us and we think it's worse than it actually is. The other way is when you see things that they're better than they actually are. Like when you are dating or with someone who you think is great but in reality they treat you badly and don't respect you. In actuality we need to see things for how they really are not any better or worse but as it is.

Someone's always going to try to one up you

No matter what the situation or where you're at someone is going to try to outdo you. Unfortunately we tend to get worked up about it and take it personally. You can't, though otherwise it will ruin your confidence. You have to remember that some people aren't going to be impressed with you and whatever you do and it can't bring you down. It's not your fault it's the way they are and it's fine. What matters is that you value yourself.

Are you attracting people around you and inviting them through body language

If you are closed off with your body language then others will feel that you're not friendly and willing to mingle. If you smile and show openness others will be more inclined to talk to you. Not everyone is going to want to talk to you but it will help get better results when doing this.

You can't take back what you say

Have you ever heard the phrase "sticks and stones may break my bones but your words will never hurt me!" This saying is truly false because our tongues are sharper than any two edged sword. Our words can affect others greatly so what we say is very important. Pause and hold back before you say something you'll regret. Cool down a bit because it can cause people to look at you in a different perspective. People often think that hey, they'll forgive me but sometimes depending on the situation people might forgive you but the damage is too great for them to want to be around you anymore. It is important to practice self control because it can help us not do things that make us regret our words and actions.

Employees value your boss and bosses value your employees.

I know for a fact this is something that is rare in the workplace. Workers don't get treated fairly and bosses don't get the respect they deserve. Good work flow comes from working in synergy in other words all working together as one. It creates the best efficiency and no one wants to do this. I also see a big lack in communication when it comes to this. People tend to keep things quiet until it gets found out about or you found at the last minute or second that it needs to be done. I've experienced this first hand and it sucks. Co-workers are fueled by each other and at the bosses. If communication and unison working could be implemented then the workplace will flourish but many times this gets overlooked and businesses do not live to their full potential.

Not everyone is going to like you.

Here is the truth about life is that everyone is not going to like you. No matter what you do and say, some people are not going to like you. This is very true that some of us want to get and grasp the result of having everyone around us admire

and like us. I had this mindset before and it's toxic because it can ruin your confidence because you have the expectation of everyone liking you and when it doesn't happen you blame yourself and lose confidence. You have to accept the

reality that not everyone is going to like and admire you and that's okay! It's a part of life and you should respect others but have a neutral mindset about them.

Don't get hung up

Never get hung up on one particular woman or guy who doesn't show you interest. If they're not interested in you then don't waste your time with them. If they like and want to be with you then they will be with you. People vote with their feet if they want to be with you then they'll make the effort to be there and want to spend time with you. After all, if you don't spend time with someone who isn't excited and wants to spend time with you. Life is too short to spend it with those who have no interest in you. Also, don't be something you're not. If you want to attract someone by being someone you don't want to be, don't do it. It ends badly for both parties because you're not being true to yourself and you're not being true to that person. It's not fair to both of you and never use someone to your advantage.

Asking for Forgiveness and walking away

In life you may run across this where you might have someone that you might have offended and the consequence is that you did something bad to hurt them. I have never been in this position but I know people who have been so I'd like to address it. When you reach out to them, you can always make amends and ask for their forgiveness if you have done something or said something to hurt them.

People often hold regret if this happens and it can be devastating knowing that in the final years of your life can have an impact knowing that you feel bad that you haven't made amends and told someone that you're truly sorry. In my belief God gave his only son that through him we will have an everlasting life by asking for forgiveness. But God can't forgive you unless you forgive others. Knowing this is important because forgiveness is an important element to human nature as we were created. Forgiving others is very important and sometimes probably the hardest thing. If they don't accept your apology it may feel bad but at least you made the attempt and that to me is an important step and a strong one because many don't have the courage to do so.

Don't Judge people based on Looks

Judging people because of the way they look or if they don't say anything is a poor way of going about in life. I ran across this issue before when I was in school many years ago in 4th grade. I remember seeing this one kid who was a bigger build and had a straight look on his face and looked like a bully or a mean kid. But I found out that he had the personality of the expression of someone who couldn't hurt a fly. We became real good friends and my judgment impulses were so off. So, I want you to take into consideration that not everyone who looks this way is a bad or grumpy person. Sometimes your senses can be spot on but until you talk to that person I wouldn't be too quick to judge. Who knows, maybe they'll be your next closest friend.

Don't bribe people into liking you

This is also an important topic about never bribing people to like you in life. When it comes to sales people tend to maybe buy them dinner or give them a little extra when closing the deal to get them to make the sale but when it comes to relationships with people it doesn't always work this way. Don't give gifts to people to get them to like you and don't give them your time if they aren't receptive to your time. Often people will send gifts to romantic interests that don't have any interest in you. It's a bad way to go. If you aren't in a relationship with someone then you shouldn't be giving them gifts. I see guys do this especially showering a woman with gifts to get them to go out with them or to keep them in a relationship that's falling apart. They lose the concept that the greatest gift you can give anyone is your time. They should have given more time to that person rather than trying to make it up in gifts. Because your time in life is limited and you can't get that time back. So, if they don't value you or your time then don't give them that attention anymore.

Getting out of our shell is the hardest thing to do.

Leaving your shell can be a very difficult task. I know for a fact everyone who wants and gets the most out of their life has to get out of the comfort/shy shell in life. If you don't then things will generally be more difficult for you. What also happens is people go in and out of their shell. I've done this where I was very outgoing and then the next time quiet as a mouse. What happens if you may not feel like saying much sometimes and that's natural but going back into your shell and staying there is not good. You'll have to force yourself out of your shell to actually make yourself an outgoing individual. Introverts have a hard time with this. I know for a fact because I used to be this way and the less socializing you do the more introverted you become. You need to push yourself out of your comfort zone. Now you don't need to start making speeches in large crowds right away but a simple hi to people to start out with wherever you are whether it's the mall, park, store, school, work, ect. You need to make baby steps and then you can take giant leaps once you get there.

Doing nothing gets you nowhere

Here's a great example of the principles many people tend to follow. They believe if I don't do anything I'll be safe in life and it may in a sense but it's most likely not going to be this way. If you don't break barriers in accomplishments and go farther in life then you're just riding the wave of the average person in life. Living this way can have effects in the long term because most people wish to be successful in their life but don't take the necessary actions and ways of life that grants this. I believe that if more people would get off their bottom and get moving instead of getting hooked on social media, trending videos, or playing video games all the time they could make the most of themselves. Make yourself more productive and discipline yourself so you can accomplish more. Many believe disciplining yourself is a bad thing but you have more freedom in your life if you discipline yourself and be more productive. It's a hard process because we tend to get hung up on our habits in our daily lives and we get comfortable with them but they never lead to success.

Conclusion:

I hope anyone who has read this book gets the full understanding and perspective of gaining confidence and becoming better in their life. I want you to succeed in every aspect in your life and remember things in life take time. Nobody is perfect and you will fall a time or two but always get back up! Don't let laziness and procrastination get in the way of your life! Prayer often works and I pray that God's will fulfills your life!

Made in the USA
Columbia, SC
25 October 2022